Sammis, Kathy
The beginning knowledge book of butterflies.
Illustrated by Paul Lipp. N.Y., MacMillan,
[1965]
unp. illus.

1.Butterflies. I.Lipp, Paul, illus.
I.Title. II.Title: Butterflies.

Butterflies

Beginning Knowledge Books are for the young reader who is eager to learn about the world around him. Beautiful color illustrations and simple words are guides that offer a wealth of carefully chosen answers for young questioners.

The editors of the Beginning Knowledge Books are grateful for the expert assistance of: Miss Amy Clampitt, Librarian, National Audubon Society, 1952-59, in checking the text; The Department of Entomology, The Connecticut Agricultural Experiment Station, for specimen material.

The Beginning Knowledge Book of Butterflies

by Kathy Sammis/Illustrated by Paul Lipp

CONTENTS

PAINTED LADY
COMMON WHITE
AMERICAN COPPER
MOURNING CLOAK
HARVESTER
GREAT SPANGLED FRITILLARY
COMMON SULPHUR
ROADSIDE SKIPPER
CABBAGE BUTTERFLY
MONARCH
GRAY HAIR-STREAK
CLOUDLESS SULPHUR
TIGER SWALLOWTAIL
WOOD NYMPH
COMMON BLUE
RED ADMIRAL
SILVER-SPOTTED SKIPPER
GIANT SWALLOWTAIL

A RUTLEDGE BOOK

 Prepared and produced for the Macmillan Company, 866 Third Avenue, New York, N.Y. 10022; Collier-Macmillan Ltd., London; Collier-Macmillan Canada, Ltd., Toronto, Ontario. Library of Congress catalog card number: 65-20622. Printed and bound by Arnoldo Mondadori, Verona, Italy.
Fourth Printing 1973

Butterflies

Butterflies live in every part of the earth where plants grow, even in the cold of the Far North. They belong to a large group of insects that also includes moths. There are more than 100,000 kinds of moths and butterflies.

There are several ways to tell moths and butterflies apart. Most butterflies fly in the daytime, most moths at night. Usually, when a butterfly is resting, it holds its wings straight up. A moth at rest holds its wings flat.

When a butterfly alights on a flower, it uncoils its spring-like tongue to reach into the flower's center and sip the sweet nectar. Butterflies usually do not eat anything else. There are even some butterflies that spend their lives without eating anything at all.

The flying stage is only one part of the life of a butterfly. It begins life as a tiny egg,  laid on a plant by a female butterfly. When the egg hatches, a tiny caterpillar  comes out.

Although at first the caterpillar is very small, it grows fast — so fast that several times it becomes too big for its skin. When this happens — usually about four times in the life of the caterpillar — the skin splits open at the back, and the caterpillar sheds it.  A new skin has grown inside the old one. This process is called molting.

When a caterpillar has reached its full growth,

it sheds its skin one last time. Then it is no longer a caterpillar, but a pupa. The pupa is enclosed in a chrysalis, or pupa case.  Only one kind of butterfly—the skipper—spins a cocoon, a silken cover, around the pupa.

The butterfly, now in the pupa stage, does not eat and hardly moves. Another change is going on. The pupa is changing from a crawling insect into a flying insect. When the change is complete, the chrysalis or pupa case splits open and the butterfly emerges.  At first its wings are soft and damp. They must dry out in the air and sunshine before the insect can fly.

Butterflies never live long. For some, the flying stage may last only a few days or a few hours.

Others may live for several months. Some go into hibernation when the weather turns cold in the fall. Others travel south, as some birds do. Though their wings are thin  and easily damaged, some butterflies are strong fliers. They may travel long distances, even over large bodies of water.

Some butterflies spend the winter in the pupa stage. Others hibernate as caterpillars. Those that do this are hatched very late in the summer. A caterpillar hatched early in the summer spends two or three weeks feeding and growing before it turns into a pupa.

In size, butterflies may be anywhere from less than 1 inch to more than 5 inches across. The giant swallowtail,  one of the largest, can be more than 5 inches across.

Painted Lady

The painted lady caterpillar has a yellow body covered with spines. It is about an inch long. It feeds on hollyhocks.

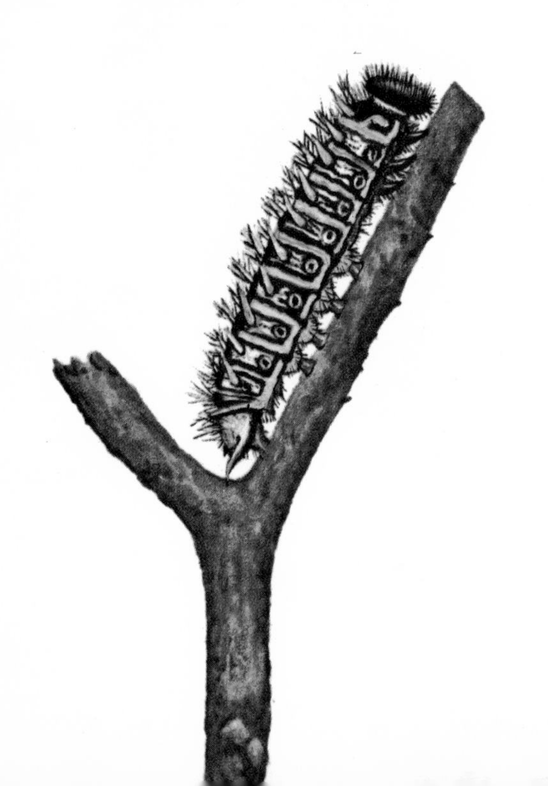

The yellowish caterpillar of the painted lady is 1¼ inches long. It is covered with spines and feeds on the spiny thistle and on hollyhocks. It makes a kind of tent by fastening together plant hairs with the silk it spins. As the caterpillar molts and grows, it must build a larger tent.

All butterflies – like all other insects – have three pairs of legs. But in one group, the brush-footed butterflies, the two front legs are small and useless. They are carried folded up under the body and the feet are like little brushes. The painted lady is one of these brush-footed butterflies.

Painted ladies gather in flocks to make long journeys. They have a wing span of 2¼ inches. The upper side of the wing is black and orange with white markings.

The painted lady has white markings on its orange and black wings. Like all brush-footed butterflies, it carries its front legs folded under its body.

Common White

The pupa case of the common white is bluish gray. A silk-like thread holds it to a bush twig.

The common white caterpillar is 1 inch long and has yellow and greenish-purple stripes. It feeds on turnip, cabbage, and mustard leaves. The bluish-gray chrysalis is attached to a piece of board or a stone by a silken thread looped around the middle. The butterfly has a wing span of 2 inches. The upper side of the wing is white marked with grayish brown. It has a rapid, zigzag flight and can often be seen in open fields.

American Copper

The American copper is often found sunning itself on a rock, its fiery wings outspread.

The American copper has a wing span of an inch or less. Yet it is a bold and fearless fighter and will attack larger butterflies. It flies rapidly, moving back and forth rather than straight ahead. It suns itself on rocks with its fiery copper wings outspread. At night it perches head downward on a grass stalk when it is ready to go to sleep.

The caterpillars, which hatch from pale green eggs in six to ten days, feed on sorrel.

Mourning Cloak

The mourning cloak butterfly lays her eggs in clusters on twigs of trees. Two weeks later, the eggs hatch into black caterpillars.

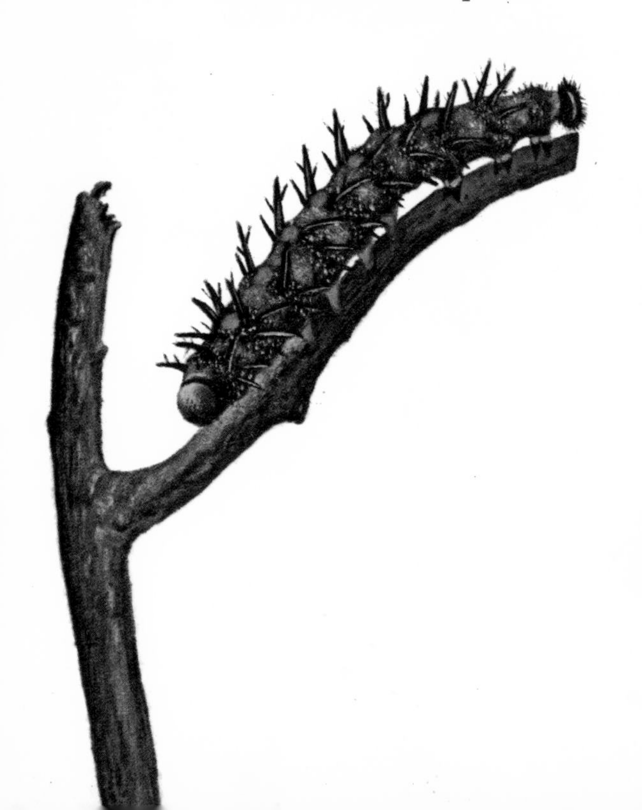

The mourning cloak butterfly lays her eggs in clusters of about twenty on elm, willow, or poplar twigs. The blackish caterpillars hatch two weeks later. They arrange themselves side by side on the nearest leaf. In the molting-growing process, they march in procession from leaf to leaf, spinning a silken carpet as they go. They separate and seek shelter beneath a stump or fence to change into the pupa, their next stage of development.

The purple-black butterfly emerges from the chrysalis in two weeks. It has a wing span of 2½ to 3 inches. Mourning cloaks gather together to sip the nectar of spoiled fruit and the sap of willow trees. In winter, mourning cloak butterflies hibernate under bridges, under loose bark, or in hollow trees.

When the mourning cloak caterpillars are ready to change into the pupa, they find shelter.
The dark purple butterfly emerges two weeks later.

Harvester

The hairy harvester caterpillar eats little insects called aphids. It becomes a pupa in two weeks.

This is the only caterpillar that eats meat. The female lays her eggs among or near aphids – tiny white insects that feed on alder trees. Three or four days later, when the caterpillars hatch, they feed on the aphids.

In two weeks, and after only three molts, the fuzzy-looking hairy caterpillar changes into the pupa. When the butterfly emerges eleven days later, it has a wing span of about 1 inch.

Great Spangled Fritillary

The great spangled fritillary hatches into a caterpillar in the spring. It eats mostly violets.

This brush-footed butterfly is found in meadows. It sucks the nectar of milkweed and snowberry. It has a wing span of 3 to 4 inches. The upper side is rusty brown. The under side is cinnamon brown with silvery spots. In the fall the female lays about 200 eggs. Two or three weeks later, when the caterpillars hatch, they eat the eggshell and go into hibernation. In the spring the caterpillars feed on violets, eating mainly at night.

Cloudless Sulphur

The eggs of the cloudless sulphur, laid on a leaf, hatch into striped caterpillars that grow to a length of $1\frac{2}{3}$ inches.

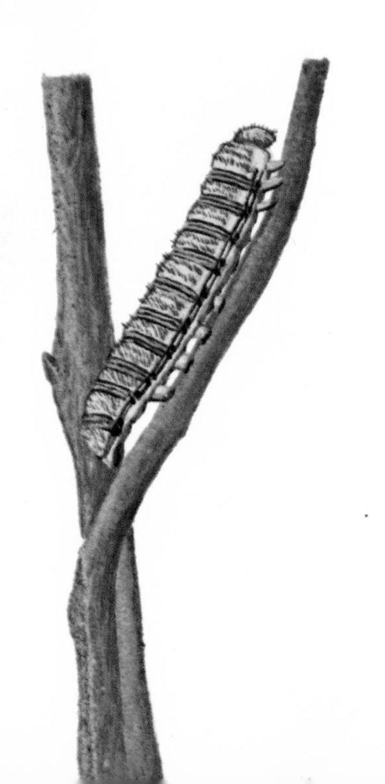

The cloudless sulphur flies with a quick, vigorous motion. Great flocks of these butterflies often travel long distances together, staying in the open sunshine.

This butterfly has a wing span of $2\frac{1}{2}$ inches. The male is a brilliant, unmarked lemon yellow and has an odor of violets. The female may be one of two colors. It may be a deep shade of orange-yellow, sometimes spotted with orange dots. The other color it may be is a pale yellow—so pale a shade that it is almost white.

The caterpillar of the cloudless sulphur is a pale yellowish green with a yellowish stripe along each side. The segments along the back appear to be stripes. It grows to $1\frac{2}{3}$ inches. It feeds on clover plants and on the leaves of the cassia tree.

The male cloudless sulphur is a brilliant, unmarked lemon yellow. The pupa, attached to a twig with a thread, shows a bulge where the wings will appear.

Roadside Skipper

The roadside skipper butterfly is black-brown on its upper side and a lilac color underneath.

When this caterpillar hatches from the pale green egg, it builds a "tent" by fastening blades of grass together with silken threads. As it molts and grows larger, it must build a larger tent. The caterpillar is covered with fine snow-white hairs and feeds on grasses.

This butterfly has a wing span of 1 inch and is blackish brown on the upper side, lilac underneath. It flies with quick starts and stops, as if skipping through the air.

Cabbage Butterfly

The green caterpillar of the cabbage butterfly feeds mainly on cabbage and cauliflower.

This butterfly has a wing span of almost 2 inches. It skips over meadows seeking the nectar of flowers. The cabbage butterfly lays its eggs on cabbage, cauliflower, or mustard leaves. The eggs are attached by a sort of glue. When the pale green caterpillars hatch a week later, they begin to eat the leaves of the plant. In two or three weeks, when they are full grown, these caterpillars have destroyed a large number of plants.

Monarch

The caterpillar of the monarch butterfly is yellowish green striped with black and yellow. It grows to a length of about 2 inches.

In the autumn, great flocks of monarch butterflies gather to begin their journey to the South. At night they rest on trees, often stopping at the same "butterfly tree" year after year.

The female monarch lays pale green, cone-shaped eggs on the undersides of milkwood leaves, one to a leaf. In three to five days the yellowish green caterpillars hatch. They change into the pupa, which has a green and gold chrysalis, in two or three weeks. The butterfly that emerges in twelve days is orange-brown with black markings and has a wing span of 4 inches.

To attract female monarchs, the male monarch gives off a perfume that smells of milkweed.

Monarch caterpillars and butterflies are not eaten by birds because they have an unpleasant taste.

The monarch butterfly emerges from a green and gold pupa case. It has black markings on its orange and brown wings. The wing span of the monarch is 4 inches.

Gray Hair-Streak

The caterpillar of the gray hair-streak becomes a butterfly with tails on its wing tips.

The gray hair-streak has a wing span of 1¼ inches. The upper wings are a dark slaty gray. The under wings are pearl gray crossed with a bold black zigzag line. There are fine, hair-like tails at the tips of its hind wings. This butterfly skips about so fast that you can hardly follow it with your eyes.

The reddish caterpillar is only ⅓ inch long. It feeds on hops and garden beans and is able to push its head inside the seed pods.

Common Sulphur

The upper side of the common sulphur's wings is bright yellow with a black border.

The common sulphur butterfly lays eggs on the clover plant. Before they hatch, the eggs turn reddish orange. The caterpillars hatch in about one week. They are grass green in color and are covered with short hairs.

About three weeks after hatching, the caterpillar fastens itself to a clover stem with a silken thread and changes into a pupa. The butterfly will emerge nine to eleven days later.

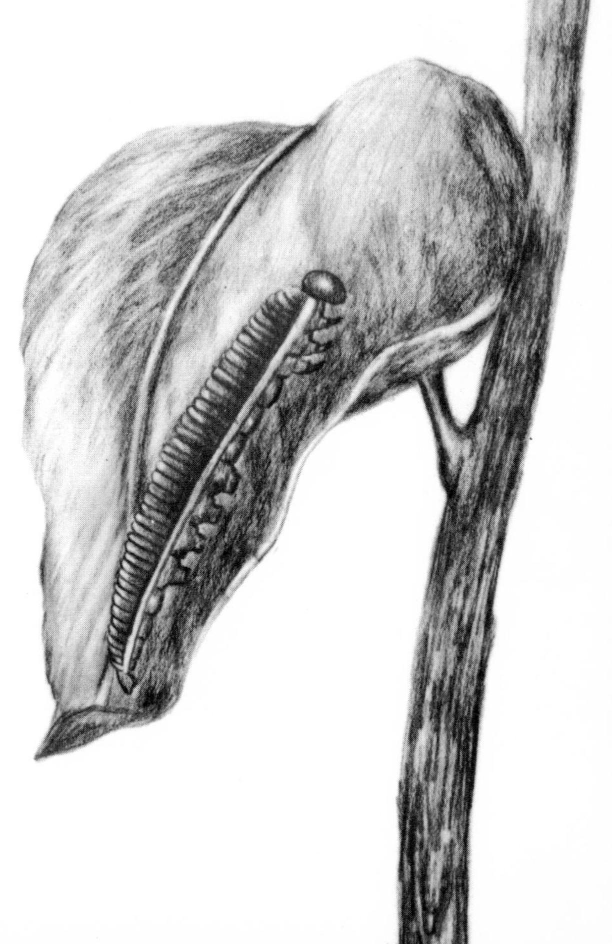

Tiger Swallowtail

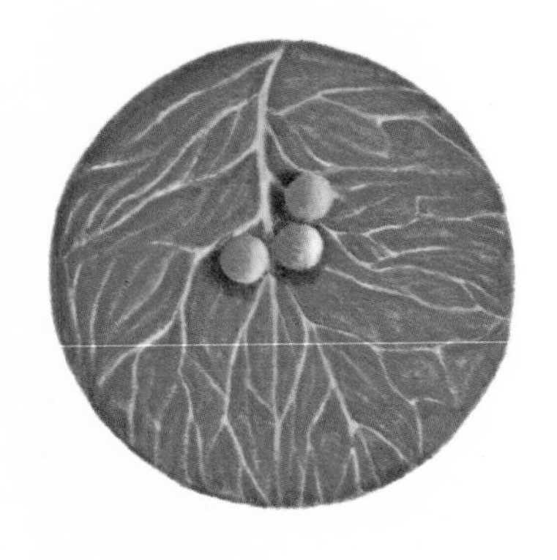

The large yellow rings and spots of the tiger swallowtail caterpillar frighten away birds and other natural enemies.

This large butterfly—3 to 5 inches —is yellow striped with black, like a tiger. Some females are almost all black. The long lower tips of the hind wings are like the tail of a swallow. The males are sometimes called "flying flowers" because they have a sweet spicy odor.

The caterpillar spins a "mattress" of silken threads on the upper side of a leaf. Before each molt, it spins a new and larger mattress. It feeds on the leaves of tulip trees, wild cherry, birch, apple, poplar, and ash. When full grown, the soft, velvety green caterpillar is 2½ inches long. The fearsome, large, yellow-ringed eye-spots on the front end of its body frighten away birds and other enemies. The yellow horns behind its head give off an unpleasant odor when it is disturbed.

The tiger swallowtail is a large butterfly with a wing span up to 5 inches wide. The male is yellow with tiger-like black stripes. Some females are black.

Wood Nymph

The green caterpillar of the common wood nymph hatches three weeks after the egg is laid.

This butterfly lays its eggs in late summer on leaves of grass. When the green caterpillars hatch three weeks later, they go immediately into hibernation. In the spring the caterpillar feeds on grass and in June when it is full grown, it changes into a pupa. The brown butterfly emerges from the chrysalis in July. It has a wing span of 1½ to 2¼ inches. Several weeks later, the female lays the eggs that will become next year's butterflies.

Common Blue

The common blue is pale rose as a caterpillar. When it becomes a butterfly, it is blue, with gray under-wings.

This butterfly lays its eggs on the flower buds of the clover, dogwood, and willow. The caterpillar, which looks white, is actually a pale rose, covered with white hair. It feeds on the nearby flowers. The caterpillar provides a sweet liquid for ants; the presence of the ants, in turn, helps to protect the caterpillar from attack by its enemies.

The common blue butterfly has a wing span of 1 inch. The wings are blue on the upper side.

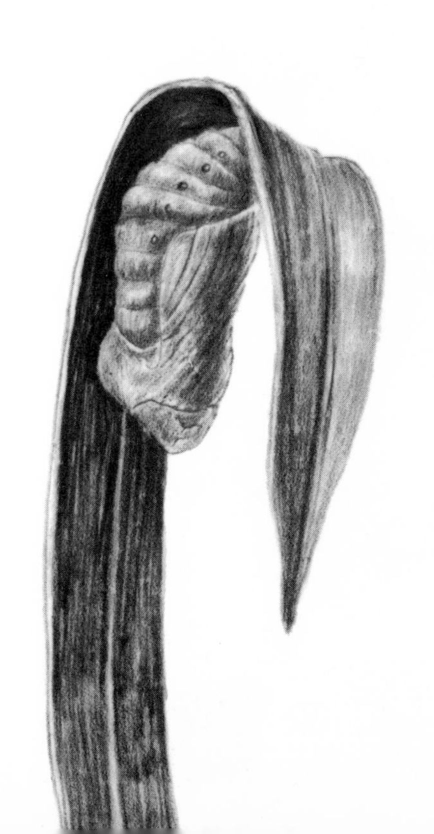

Red Admiral

To protect itself, a red admiral caterpillar forms a tent-like shelter of nettle leaves and silk thread.

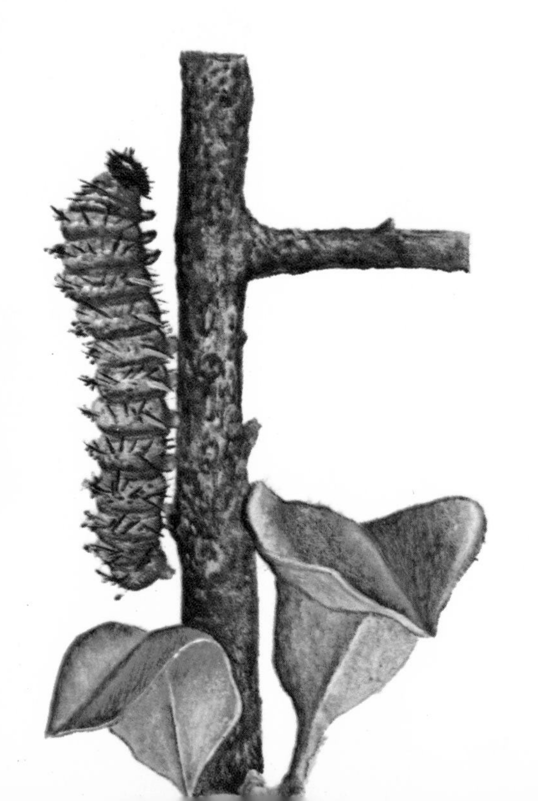

The red admiral butterfly has purple-black wings streaked with orange-red and spotted with white. It has a wing span of 2 inches.

The red admiral caterpillar protects itself from bad weather and enemies by forming a tent-like shelter of nettle leaves fastened with silken threads. It lives in this "tent" about a week, until its first molt. After molting, it eats the old nest and proceeds to build a larger one. This process is repeated until it is full grown – the chrysalis is often formed within the last "tent."

This butterfly is found in shaded woodland and at the edges of forested swamps. It may rest on a tree trunk or sun itself on a rock or log with outspread wings. It sucks the liquid from overripe plums and pears and the sap from trees.

The purple-black wings of the red admiral butterfly
are dotted with white and streaked in orange-red.
The red admiral is found in shady woods and swamps.

Silver-Spotted Skippe

The silver-spotted skipper has a wing span of up to 2 inches. It flies with a skipping motion.

The silver-spotted skipper darts about quickly—it seems to skip. It has a wing span of 1¾ to 2 inches. The upper side is brown with patches of yellow; the under side of each hind wing has a patch of white.

The skipper caterpillar builds a tent-like shelter by fastening two leaves together with silken threads. At night the caterpillar crawls out of its "tent" to eat locust leaves.

The skipper is the only butterfly caterpillar that spins a cocoon.

Giant Swallowtail

Dots and splashes of yellow mark the rich brown wings of the beautiful swallowtail butterfly.

The giant swallowtail is the largest butterfly in the United States —it has a wing span of 4 to 5½ inches. The upper sides of its wings are a rich brown with yellow spots; the under sides are yellow. It has "tails" on its hind wings.

In the South the caterpillar is called the "orange dog" because it eats the leaves of orange trees.

When the insect is disturbed, scent pouches behind its head give off an unpleasant musky odor.